Hello Me, Where Am I?

Hello Me, Where Am I?

*The Brutally Honest and Raw
Emotional Stories of an Addict on the
Path of Recovery and Discovery*

Kevin Kaminski

Library of Congress Control Number: 2018908894
ISBN: Hardcover   978-1-9845-2531-4
                  Softcover   978-1-9845-2530-7
                  eBook   978-1-9845-2529-1

Rev. date: 02/04/2019

To order additional copies of this book, contact:
Xlibris
1-888-795-4274
www.Xlibris.com
Orders@Xlibris.com
766561

Kevin wrote this book before taking his life on December 10, 2015. Kevin, your book has been Completed, but your legacy of helping those in need continues.

Strength, Determination, Merciless Forever... SDMF

The completion of this book is dedicated to
Kevin Lawrence Kaminski

We love and miss you,
Kelly, Kylen, and Keely

Rest in peace
6/6/1969-12/10/2015

Contents

Preface

I am Kevin, and I am an alcoholic and addict in recovery!

I can finally see the truth. I was a train, a mighty locomotive. There was no track I could not travel. There was no hill that I could not climb. I was fast, I was strong, and I was powerful.

But on August 22, 2013, I derailed!

I was very lucky that the alarm sounded, and I had enough time to avoid a deadly and devastating crash. I still took on plenty of damage, but the damage was nothing compared to the pain, the agony, and the total devastation that I was leaving behind me. Emotional, psychological, and real damages lay everywhere like bodies in the fields of a battlefield during the Civil War. I believe that I never truly looked back to see the mayhem. My disease blinded me from the horrors. My Machiavellian lifestyle was vicious and hurtful, and worst of all, I didn't care who or what I was destroying. I took care of me at any cost. Reflecting back, I did a lot of good deeds, but many were for the wrong reasons.

I am on a journey of recovery and discovery. I have taken my once-mighty locomotive off the track and put it into the station, out of commission, down for repairs, taking a time-out. I need to be fixed and healed so that I have a chance to get back up and running the way I would really like to be running—changed for the better—to get out of the station healthy and renewed with a new moral compass and sense of direction. I am excited to get back on track—only this time, I will be traveling more rewarding new tracks.

I can still see the destroyed old twisted track in my rearview mirror, and I can't change that. I can attempt to repair that track so that I may be able to bring my new train back into those stations, but that will take time and patience.

I want to be fixed today or tomorrow! I don't want to have to work for it; I just want it to happen! Why can't I just wave my magic wand and make it right?

Insanity! It took me twenty-five years to tie this track into a twisted, grotesque, and complicated web. It will take a little more than two days, two weeks, two months, and possibly even two years or more to untangle it.

These are my stories. They are real, they are brutally honest, and they are my raw emotions—emotions ranging from angry, anxious, and depressed to happy, relieved, and joyful. This is a painful yet extremely rewarding journey—a journey that many can relate to and unfortunately a journey many have taken. If you have ever been there, wherever "there" is, you will understand. If you are sick or have ever been sick, know that there is hope. If you have taken off your mask or even if you continue to wear your masks, you will relate. Hopefully these stories—these gut-wrenching stories—will comfort you in the fact that you are not alone. All are sick; some are sicker than others.

My clarity has given me the opportunity to open up my once cloudy mind and put words onto a blank piece of paper. My pen and fingers can't keep up with my mind. It is as if something or someone has taken over control of my hands. I am having an out-of-body experience, just sitting back and watching the words appear. The pen is flying. The keyboard is sparking. It is truly awesome and amazing to sit back and watch. Could it just be me inside—the old creative me—that has been buried under a blanket of this awful disease?

I hope you too can read and relate and get on a path. Take your own journey of recovery and discovery. Take the first step, become aware, and gain hope in the fact that you are never alone!

Have faith and hope that there is a new beginning waiting for you!

Maybe, just maybe, you too will find out where you are!

Love-Hate Relationship

I met her when I was young, carefree, and full of life. She is exciting, daring, and just my type. We fell in love, and nothing could separate us—nothing! She is the love of my life. She is my soul mate. With her by my side, I can go anywhere and do anything. I feel immortal when I am with her. She is the life of the party, she is the envy of everyone's eyes, and she is all mine, and we will be together forever. Nothing will get in between us—nothing. Our lives will never be apart. We have become one!

It seems that the honeymoon is over. She has become very demanding, and she has some major control issues. She is like a puppet master, and I am her puppet. She has begun to control my every move. She has become very jealous. She wants me all the time, she doesn't want me seeing others, and she is becoming uncontrollable.

However, she is so beautiful, and when I'm with her, nobody else matters. She is everything to me. She seems to always get her way, yet I still love her and never want to be away from her. I thought I was selfish, but she defines the very meaning of the word! When it's her time, watch out and give her your full attention or else. This is her world. I just live in it. She will always, and I mean always, get her way!

She is so inviting, and her companionship is so soothing. She builds up my courage, she gives me the strength of one hundred men, and she makes me feel as if I am walking on air. Nothing else matters when I am with her—nothing. I love her so damn much!

She never tells me the truth. She is always lying, and she is so deceitful. She always gets me in trouble. I don't know where, I don't know when, I don't know why, and I don't know how, but I know she will ruin me in the end. Why won't she just let me be me? Why do

I have to change? Why does she always have to tell me what to do? Why do I love her so? Why?

She always says sorry. I know she means it, but there is something behind her words that tells me she will do it again. Empty promises are all I feel. I want to stay with her, but she is destroying my life. She can never be trusted. She will never change! I think she is losing it. She is baffling and unmanageable, and I must get away from her. Leave her before she hurts me or possibly even kill me. I am scared of her!

I have been with her for so many years. She is everything to me—everything! We have been together for so many wonderful, crazy, and spontaneous adventures. We have traveled the world together. I don't know how to live without her. We have been life partners. How can I even contemplate leaving her? I love her, and she loves me. Sure we have our problems. All relationships have problems. We can see a counselor, we can work together, and we can get through these rough waters—together. I can't leave her; she means so much to me. There isn't anything that we can't solve or conquer together!

She doesn't want the help. She wants to continue playing, destroying, and being the puppet master. She has no desire to be controlled. I am powerless to her every move. She has a will of her own, and she will never change—never!

I can't have her anymore; she must be out of my life. I am scared to be alone—without my partner, without my soul mate. I am afraid of the changes. Whom will I meet? What will I do? Who will be there for me when I need her? What will life look like without her? I am blind and numb, for she has taken away my sight, my spark, and my feelings. I don't know how to live without her. She is and always will be a part of me. I miss her already. I wish she would have never changed. Why can't we go back to the way we were in the beginning? Together, we had so many wonderful memories yet so many tragic endings. Why, O God, why can't we make this relationship work? I don't know if life will ever be the same without her!

I love her, and at the same time, I hate everything about her. She is my friend, she is my partner, she is my shortfall, and she is my worst nightmare.

She is alcohol!

Together, we have a *love-hate relationship.*

I Am Sick!

I am running and gunning!

I am driven and successful!

I am wanted and needed!

I am superman and an immortal!

I am superman in a dark, lonely corner, balled up in the fetal position, trying to hang onto life, fighting to find a rope to pull me out of this darkness, grasping for every breath, and drowning in a sea of hopeless thoughts and actions. I am waiting to be taken but going nowhere as if caught in quicksand in the middle of a very lonely dry, hot desert.

I realize that I am sick, but I am lucky, for I am still alive!

How did "it" vanish so quickly? Where did "it" go? Why did "it" abandon me? What did I do to lose "it"?

I don't even know what "it" is!

Judgment begins. It comes very swiftly. It is very uneducated and very unwanted, and judgment doesn't stop coming. Judgment has just begun. Worst fears are realized. Humility, vulnerability, shame, and guilt are feeding on me like sharks in a sea of blood.

The people mean well. They genuinely care, but they just don't understand. I don't even understand, so how could they? Yet they persist with their questions, their stares, and their gossip. They all think they have "it," they all want me to get "it" back, and they will stop at nothing to ensure I am choking down any and all ideas to get "it" back and becoming me again.

4

But who am I?

To each, I am different—a beautiful collection of masks all painted with sincerity, confidence, and individual touch. Each mask, on its own and to its owner, is the perfect match. Each mask is just another sophisticated facade that hides the sickness of addiction, depression, and anxiety. On the outside, I may seem like the statue or the rock—someone who is calm, cool, and in complete control. The outsider would be led to think these attributes are true because all they are seeing is my collection of ever-changing and ever-concealing masks. My masks are like a self-built prison—a prison that is made up of impenetrable walls to protect me from any harm but also to keep me from being able to liberate my true self.

I am too proud to take off the masks. I continue to slowly suffocate on the belief that "it" is just around the corner. I don't need anyone to find "it." I have always stood alone yet never alone. I haven't spent a day of my life alone. I have always had God and those who have supported me at my side.

The glares, the whispers, and worst of all, the silence all equal weapons of destruction and tools of hypocrisy.

Analyzing, healing, and criticizing were all attempts to find "it." Don't they realize that there is nothing I can do about the events of the past? Those stories, those memories, those mistakes, and those horrors are etched in stone—never to be changed or erased but only to be referenced to and learned from, hoping slowly, painfully slowly, for them to fade away with time and never to be felt again but never to be forgotten, like the etched names of our loved ones upon their graves, slowly fading away.

However, none of them are really talking to me. All of them are just talking to their mask, or could it truly be a mirror? Are most of them feeling just as guilty and trying to find "it" themselves? Maybe they aren't who they appear to be at all. Couldn't it just be possible that they, as well, are wearing masks?

Could it be that we all walk around in life as if we are always dressed for a masquerade ball, constantly living in fear and scared to show ourselves to anyone and everyone?

All are sick; some are sicker than others.

This thought gives me strength; this idea gives me hope. We are all in this life together, trying to find "it" even though none of us truly knows what "it" is.

Maybe I am on track to finding "it" because I had the courage to take off my mask and let them see the vulnerability that lies beneath. Vulnerability bears strength. Education is my weapon, and my support system is my armor. I am prepared for the challenge of regaining "it"!

I am scared of "it"!

I am excited about finding "it"!

I am not alone fighting for "it," never alone!

But most of all,

I am sick!

Me versus Myself and I!

I am in the fight for my life. This fight will be vicious and brutal, and it will never have an end. I am going to definitely take some heavy blows and receive a large amount of damage. However, when I get knocked down, I must be resilient and pick myself off the mat in order to continue to fight.

No ten counts here!

Remember, it is not the size of the man in the fight that counts, it is the size of the fight in the man that truly matters and of which will have the most profound effect on the results.

However, I am not only in this fight against the disease of addiction. Addiction doesn't fight alone. Addiction is cunning, baffling, and very powerful. Addiction is tactful enough to gain an ally in this war, a very powerful and influential ally—myself! But it's not just myself, though. This self that I am fighting is not a healthy self but a very sick and hurting self—a self that is injured and cornered and will do anything to anybody at any time to get out of that situation. Yes, my sickness is accompanied by my ego, and it is this ego that has become part of my weakness. Addiction sees this and takes the opportunity to seize this ally through that very weakness. Addiction and my ego have now become one and are teamed up to fight me to my death.

It is now me versus myself and I.

One of the biggest roadblocks that addicts like me are up against is the fact that I am under the delusion that I am in total control of the situation and that there is nothing wrong—my ego's perspective on the situation. The delusion that I am on the top of my game makes it impossible for me to want to change. This is a very complicated problem because my ego will not let me admit that there exists a flaw in this perfect system of me. All systems are go. I am a god in my world. In my world, people worship me and nothing can stop me and my swelled-up ego. It is preposterous to think that there is something broken or sick inside me.

Don't fix what is not broken, right?

Well, note to self, take the glasses of disease and ego off and notice that reality shows us that I derailed this train many miles ago. It's just that this dynamic duo of destruction, the addiction and ego, are in control of my motives. Maybe not all my motives are under this insidious control, but the majority of them are.

This strategic disease is also remarkably skilled at using selective amnesia and controlling my memory. It allows me to forget all the pain, suffering, and shame that accompany my addiction, and then at the same time, it glorifies and rewards the perceived good times and comfortable feelings of the experiences.

So these two, the disease of addiction and my sick and delusional ego, are working hand in hand to construct barbed-wire fences, brick walls, steel curtains, and insurmountable obstacles—all of them being built to protect them from being discovered.

These out-of-control puppet masters take away my sight. They won't allow my eyes to see the supporting hands that are being reached out to help me. They have convinced me that there is no trouble, problem, or chaos in my life. Therefore, without any apparent problems in my disillusioned life, there is no reason to seek a solution—a solution that this dynamic duo of death knows will result to the destruction of themselves. Hence, it is self-preservation that causes them to hide the truth.

In order to begin to heal and fight against them, I must deflate this tremendously out-of-proportion ego and loosen the grasp of this horrible disease. Without these two factors being identified and brought into the light, they will continue to grow and grow and gain more and more control until they work toward their imminent goal.

The ruthless and ugly death of me!

So why is it so hard for me to kill this ego that I have birthed? Why have I gone through so much time and effort feeding my ego and letting it get out of control? Is society to blame? Why the insistent need to be worshipped and to be powerful and wealthy?

Status and power are both weapons that my ego wields with deadly accuracy. These two, along with money, have all proven in excess to have an absolutely devastating role in my life. Yet I do everything and anything to gain them, and I mean everything and anything!

An absolute catch-22!

Acquire them in excess, and I will surely die because of how my ego and I handle them. Don't acquire them, and I don't feel like I am living. Damned if I do, damned if I don't. This is surely nurture, not nature, at its very core. In excess, status, power, and money create chaos in my world. Society goes after them all so that we can gain more and more control and feed our egos. My ego is like a fat big muddy pig at the trough, eating it up as fast as it can get it. *Oink, oink,* says my ego as it puts its snout into this slop of life.

To stand a chance at winning this war, I must deflate this enlarged ego. I must rewire myself and change! I must get back to the basics and go after more rewarding goals—goals that will reward me internally and spiritually, not monetarily. Hope, faith, charity, and love shall replace the old narcissistic goals. Anonymity and internal peace shall break me from the chains of bondage and set me free—set me free to gain a much healthier lifestyle. Sure, it is a lifestyle that doesn't seem as exciting, doesn't feel normal, and one that goes against the grain of the sick majority's vision, but it is a lifestyle that truly goes after much, much more rewarding and safer goals.

KISS (keep it simple, stupid). Time to simplify my life and get back to the basics. Time to cure myself of the disease of "more."

Honestly, when is enough enough?

When status, power, and money are the goals—never! It is time to stop chasing the pot of gold at the end of the rainbow and let the colors of the rainbows be the goal. Time to sit back and take in the beauty of such an amazing natural phenomenon and to stop the craziness that ensues when chasing the myths of the gold.

Change? I don't like change. I won't change. I can't change!

Why is it that I instantly become a mule when I'm being pulled in the direction of change? It must be the disease once again controlling me and turning me into a stubborn, defiant, and immovable creature. With my heels dug in and my weight shifted backward, I just can't allow myself to be budged.

I feel trapped—trapped like a bug that is caught in a lampshade. A bug is attracted to the radiant heat that is thrown off by light. It enjoys the feeling that it receives from it. I, too, am attracted to the feelings that my addiction gives me. A bug will do anything to get to that radiant heat, and I as well will lie, cheat, and steal to get to my addiction.

Take for example the lights in the ceiling with a cover over them. The bugs work their way into this little space in order to gain this comforting warmth. They enjoy this warmth so much that they don't even realize the danger that they are in. The joy and elation that they are enjoying mask the heat that is slowly killing them. They are literally cooking themselves because they don't realize through the good times what is truly happening around them in their environment. They are oblivious to the important things that matter because their body and mind are being controlled by what they want, not what they need.

The disease of "more"!

Addiction is controlling my mind and distracting me from the dangerous environment that I have around me. I am like these bugs going toward the light, and like those bugs without some intervention, I will slowly cook myself and die. Absolutely baffling and powerful!

In order to live, I must change. And I must change now!

Change is the thing that I fear the most. I am comfortable with the norm. The norm gives me that warm, cozy feeling of the heat from the light. But remember, that is the heat that is killing me, slowly but surely. To change takes me out of my comfort zone. I don't have the same level of control during change. With the norm, I am king, my ego controls the moves, and I know when to zig and when to zag. When I invite change, I am off-balance. The zigs are when I needed to zag; the zags are needed when I zig. Turmoil, fear, uneasiness, and anxiety all come along with change.

No wonder I don't like it. Who wants a heavy dose of any of these negative emotions? However, I must change! I must look at change directly in the eyes and face it like my life matters on it, because it does. I know that if I don't change, my sobriety date will! I need to embrace these absolutely awkward emotions and take them head on. Time to get out of my comfort zone and into the frying pan just out of the reach of the flames. It is time for me to feel the heat, to actually begin to feel, to end being numb to my surroundings, to be aware of the heat, and to know when too much is dangerous to my well-being.

How, what, why, where, when, and whom do I change?

Immediately, everything will have a purpose if I want to survive and give myself the best opportunity to make it. I change everything—what I do, where I go, and whom I am with, and most importantly, I change my motives. It is also mandatory that I change my expectations of others, and most importantly, I change the expectations I have of myself.

Expectations breed resentments.

Resentments feed hate and anger.

Expectations can lead to hate and anger!

Resentments are a remarkably interesting phenomenon. I hold the resentment because somebody or something has upset me and has not met my expectations. So the resentment becomes like poison. Now I want the individual who failed me to suffer, so I am in possession of this poison. Now that individual doesn't care, and they probably don't even know that they have done anything wrong, so they go on with no ill feelings. So here I am with the poison, getting myself sick over the situation. The moral of the story is that resentments are like drinking poison in hopes that someone else will get sick!

I must remember that I am human, and so are others. Stop judging and start living. People are not perfect, and I don't have to try to be perfect during this time of transition or really for the time beyond. I need to make sure that my side of the street is clean and let others take care of their trash.

I need to shake it up and let life roll, like the roll of the dice during craps—sometimes the numbers add up to a win, sometimes they are neutral, and sometimes they lose. I, too, will see successes, neutrality, and failures. I must have the intestinal fortitude to carry on, pick the dice back up, and roll them again if they don't land on success.

I need to make the changes that will lead me to safety and serenity and away from the deadly heat of the light.

I must have the tenacity to drive these new changes into my life in order to win the battle of *me versus myself and I!*

Together

I am sick. You are sick. We are all sick!

We are never alone, and all have some support, and yet others have even more support. Nonetheless, we all have one another.

As we gather here together, I judge, you judge, we judge, and we are judged.

I am sick. You are sick. We are all sick.

I judge myself, and I don't let up. I am harder on myself than any other person could possibly be. I am always beating on myself like a member of a chain gang, hammering away at the rocks on the yard.

Why is there this relentless struggle for perfection?

How am I feeling? What range of emotions am I dealing with today? What is my emotional goal today? What am I even doing here?

How do I answer questions that I fear like the angel of death itself?

Am I the sickest person here because I am still hiding behind my mask? I am consumed by fear among total strangers, sick strangers, yet I still don't have the courage or the ability to feel and take off my mask. Why, oh why, can't I just put down my guard, walk away from this fight, and surrender to what is truly at the core of my existence? Why?

Is it because I am too afraid to find myself, or could it just be the disease attempting to keep its cold, heartless claws dug into my very essence of being?

I am sick. You are sick. We are all sick.

Like an old-time Western wagon train, we started off alone on this open trail—weak, separate, trembling, and barely breathing or speaking. We are all scared, anxious, embarrassed, and overwhelmed with the possibilities of where this trail may lead us. We don't even know where the wagon train is going or how we even got involved in it. We do know, however, that together, we are stronger, more secure, and much safer. If the Indians attack us, like our peers, with their harmful arrows and deadly spears, we are being attacked with such ugly forms of weapons, such as the stares, the gossip, and the judgments. We must defend one another and circle the wagons.

We are stronger together!

If one of us strays from the wagon train, they are in danger of being attacked. However, the day will come when we will all need to leave the comfort and safety of the wagon train. When that time comes, we will need to be brave, capable, and clear minded. We will drive away to establish our own homesteads and lives. Although we can't build our homesteads in isolation, we must do our best to not be alone. We must establish a homestead that has stable, understanding, and knowledgeable homes within a safe distance. A support system must be near us for safety, positive reinforcement, and comforting reassurance.

In this institution, this group of healing individuals have come together via totally different trails and all with tremendously different stories. Each story can only be told by that individual. They are completely unique stories like the people that tell them. I am just one of these people. I must recognize that I am like one small cog in this engine we call life. It takes many cogs and various parts to make this engine run. This engine doesn't always run smoothly, nor does it have to in order to be effective. It just needs to keep on running, and when some of its cogs break, the engine needs to get them fixed to perform at its peak.

It is also important to realize that I don't have to keep this machine running by myself. I have you and you have me and we together have others. And this makes you and me that much more valuable to each other than you can imagine. Cogs break. I am a cog, and I am broken. I can and will be fixed. If this engine wants to perform at its peak, then all its cogs and parts must be working together like an orchestra—an orchestra made up of several musicians, each sounding wonderful alone but put them together and you have a powerful and beautiful arrangement. The whole is greater than the sum of all parts.

I am here because I finally am sick and tired of being sick and tired. I have surrendered to myself and to the thought of ever being able to be in control if I don't make a change. I have dropped the gloves and am willing to give up this absolutely futile fight. My arms are tired, my body is bruised, and my heart is aching. I do feel blessed, however, because at least I am having these aches and pains. These aches and pains give me the best news of all—the news that I am feeling, therefore, that I am still alive!

I still have a chance to heal.

So here we are—rusty, broken cogs and parts of this engine, tired, sore, and beaten up fighters. Be glad we are not "there" anymore. We are where we need to be: together and healing.

I am in a place that can help me and find me—a place where I am with you so it will help all of us find ourselves. Together.

Together, we are stronger, more secure, and safer.

Let us not see this time together as a time of weakness, humiliation, and shame. Let us rejoice during this awakening. Let us be proud of our bold decision to allow someone to grab ahold of us and help us along the trail, to pick us up off the canvas, and to assist us on this grueling journey.

I am sick. You are sick. We are sick.

This is just another chapter in the book of life, a beginning to a most beautiful story. Let us take these first steps together.

Remember, together we are stronger, more secure, and safer.

This is an unknown trail; hold my hand, and I will hold yours.

Know that we go nowhere if we don't take the first step!

So tread lightly, but be steadfast upon the trail—each one of us on our own trail, each one's trail unknown to the other. No matter what happens, may all our stories end up with happy endings.

I want to thank you for being here for me and, again, more importantly, being here for you.

There is comfort in the fact that we are here, *together!*

Can I Cry?

Can a statue cry?

Statues are made of marble, granite, and metal. Statues are stoic and reliable. The world needs statues. They have their purpose. Statues are strong, unemotional, and solid.

Statues can't cry!

Can a rock cry?

The world needs rocks—something or, more importantly, someone to grab ahold of when the angry, rushing river of emotions has got you in its grasp. Rocks are strong, unemotional, and solid.

Rocks can't cry!

I have trained my entire life to be the statue and to be the rock to avoid tears, to avoid weakness, and to abandon my defenselessness. I need to be strong, unemotional, and solid.

Cry? It isn't what big boys do. Big boys don't cry! From the beginning of time, we are taught that when we experience pain, rub a little dirt on it.

Stop before you begin.

However, nobody sat this little boy down and told him—before he became a big boy—the difference between pain and emotional suffering. The emotions I was taught and was able to convey included but were not limited to being happy, sad, mad, scared, and silly—concrete, emotionless emotions that we can all understand, emotions that we can rub a little dirt on or receive some candy with to make them go away. Now that I am older, candy is dandy, but liquor is quicker. I relate candy to happiness, gratification, and childhood innocence. Today give me liquor, and I can have all these wonderful feelings faster, and the good feelings will never go away.

Says the spider to the fly.

Tears are weakness, guilt, and vulnerability. I don't know what these feelings are. I don't have these emotions that others experience. I see the weak, the sick, and the lowly cry. I am not armed for that battle from the very beginning. If I experience these, I will have brought a knife to a gunfight. I will have lost every time.

But wait, I think I have those emotions . . . No, it must be something else.

Why can't I breathe? Why do I gasp? What is wrong with me?

Big boys don't cry!

Stop, breathe, and regain your composure. Remember, I am the statue. I am the rock. Do not let frailty and instability rear their ugly heads from behind your mask.

Continue on, O mighty soldier. Continue to suppress the unknown. Continue to bury the emotional volcano that is going to eventually erupt from within.

Don't get out of the boat. Go down with the ship. Be strong, be unemotional, and be solid.

But I am sick, and I am human. I am not strong. I do have emotions, and I am not very solid.

However, like the statue and the rock, I still can't cry!

I continue to tell myself that it is all right to take off my mask. It is safe to show the real me—the me that is hiding in the corner, lost and scared. All those around me are begging me to stop repressing these feelings and to let them out. I really want to, but I just don't know how to. I don't even know what these feelings are, let alone how to handle them. I am trying to play a game with rules I don't know. I desperately want to win this game. Well, really, I just want to be able to participate in this game. It is so difficult and so unnatural, and it feels so foreign and wrong to me. But why would it be wrong? Wouldn't it just be different? Could it possibly be more right than I realize?

I am told that tears are very healing. Tears take out the toxins that can be held up inside. Tears are actually a big part of the healing process. Tears aren't bad, tears aren't wrong, and tears are actually there to help me.

I have repressed these feelings and numbed myself for so long—all so that I didn't have to feel them. Now they are asking me to stop the numbing and begin feeling. Be that as it may, it still hurts and it is still scary.

Yes, showing emotions and crying are scary and somewhat awkward, but I must faithfully remember that these are a very important function of the healing process. I must be able to feel in order to heal. I do my best to try to fake it until I make it. Tears arrive, but they are not real tears. They are more like tears of effort and strain. Real tears of emotion just can't be obtained at this point in time. I continue to work on taking off my masks. I continue to tell myself that it is all right and that I can step away from the shore and into the water. There are lifeguards to keep me safe, just as there are people in my life to support me during this challenging time. So I must trust and have faith that these steps will not cause me harm. I go ahead and step away.

Tears of pain, tears of sorrow, and tears of shame begin to flow—tears that come with absolutely no warning. The floodgates have opened, and it seems that a sea of emotions have been released. The dam of denial has been finally broken.

I am relieved yet still scared, but more importantly, I am finally and honestly feeling. Those around me are supportive, and they comforted as well. They can now see the me, the real me, the little boy that is scared and lonely. They put me in their arms and comfort me during my time of need. The tears have seemed to take some of the venom that has been held up inside and have extracted it out of my soul, away from my body, so that this poison can no longer cause me harm.

It has been difficult but rewarding. I have been able to dig down deep and pull out emotions that have been repressed for years, and finally, I can answer the question, *Can I cry?*

Who Is Driving?

I am the driver of this bus!

I am the captain of this ship!

I am the conductor of this train!

Or am I?

Who is honestly in charge of where I am going and what treasures or dangers I am heading toward?

Seriously, I don't control anything. I am human, and I am sick. I need to stop grabbing onto the wheel and steering it toward imminent danger.

But if I let go of the wheel, then who will drive? Who will be steering? Where will I go? What might go wrong?

But wait, what might possibly go right?

It is time to let go and grab the faith and honesty that I truly never had control in the first place. My selfish, narcissistic, and self-centered thoughts would like me to believe that I was in control, but I have news for me. I have always been the passenger.

Now I find myself staring at a crossroad in life. It is time for me to make a choice—a difficult, scary, and heroic choice, a choice that just might save my life!

I must surrender to my own self-will, for it has put me in constant danger. I must now make a life-altering decision on whom I want to be my driver. Do I want a disease or a Higher Power at my controls?

This is an easy decision one would think, but this decision is far from simple and carefree. There are several emotions and motives that are hidden. These emotions and motives will need to be discovered, then they will all need to be weighed and measured so that they can help me make an educated decision—the decision.

If I choose the disease, I can find comfort in my surroundings, I can find it to be a very rough road, and I can find my past. I would not need a GPS because I have traveled these roads for a lifetime. However, almost all these roads have led me to some forms of danger and/or negative consequences.

If I choose faith, I can find comfort in God's presence. I can find it to be a very smooth road, yet I will struggle to find my past. Therefore, I won't know my way around, and I will need to stop and ask for directions. But come on, whom am I trying to kid? I don't stop and ask for directions. It is not what I do. I am in charge. To actually reach out and ask for help? Unheard of. I wonder whom, what, or how I would even ask for directions. But these roads don't seem to be as dangerous. Intimidating, yes, but dangerous, no. And best of all, there are hope and positive consequences at the end of these roads.

My whole life, I have been going through a tunnel with my eyes fixed upon the light at the end of it. I never realized or wanted to believe that with disease as my conductor, the light at the end of the tunnel is an oncoming train barreling directly toward me like a missile, and I was just waiting for the crash and devastation.

With God, my higher power, as my conductor, I must believe and have faith that the light at the end of the tunnel is a beacon of hope, a beacon of light, showing me the way to a better, safer, and more enjoyable life—a life that I can cherish, a life that I and my family will be proud of.

Again, I ask myself, Why is there even a debate?

There is only one clear choice, so why is it so hard to make this decision?

Because I must remember that I am sick—very sick and very confused. My disease would like me to forget all the negative consequences but remember all the good times. My disease wants me to walk along the lines of insanity without realizing that I am in danger.

I don't want to drive off a cliff!

Then why, oh why, do I continue to let this disease be the driver of my life?

Because I am sick, very sick!

By being brutally honest, steadfast, and strong, I shall pry the cold, vicious, and violent hands of disease from my wheel and give my controls over to faith, hope, and God, my higher power. I realize that this task will be no walk in the park. The concept is very simple, but the task itself will be very difficult. It will take patience and time. I must practice progress rather than perfection. Remember, I am human, so I will make mistakes.

I have learned, realized, and surrendered to the fact that I was never in control. I will do my best in the future to not attempt to take over the controls again with my self-will. I already know how the ending to that story goes.

I will pray with all my heart to the heavens that faith, hope, and God, my higher power, can and will gain control of me and save my life, for now I know *who is driving.*

Hunt or Be Hunted

A Story of Honesty and Deception

Can I truly be honest with myself?

Will I continue to try to deceive myself?

Is this going to be the same old song and dance?

I am the boy who cries wolf! Similar to that story, my wolf is real—it is the big bad wolf, and its name is addiction!

Who's afraid of the big bad wolf, the big bad wolf, the big bad wolf?

I am!

The wolf may seem defeated, and it may stop attacking after it has been fired upon. But if I, the sheep, forget that the wolf is out in the woods and I don't keep an eye on it, it will come back, stronger, smarter, and angrier, and it won't quit coming until it has eaten me.

I can't simply chase the wolf away; I must hunt it down and kill it before it kills me!

The wolf just attacked, and once again, I have scared it away. I am the ashamed and guilt-ridden sheep. So the next move is mine to make.

Or is it?

Do I truly have the clarity, the brutal honesty, and the courage to hunt down the big bad wolf? Or will the wolf win again and come back to feed on the defenseless sheep?

It is time for me to become a lion and not for the herd but for me. I must dig deep past the lies, the deception, and the empty promises that this disease has offered me. I must change, and I must stop being the hunted and must now become the hunter! I must be tenacious, courageous, and relentless until this wolf—this monster, this demon—is dead!

Can I look in the mirror and be open and brutally honest? I am concerned. I can't do this task with others around me. So I wonder, Can I at least look in the mirror while I am all by myself?

Thanks to my disease, I don't do brutal honesty—let alone any form of honesty—well. Honesty is a game that I have rarely played. I have looked in that mirror for decades, and I have put on my mask of deception to deflect any of the hurt, harm, pain, and devastation that the sick me has brought forth.

To end these negative consequences is exactly why brutal honesty has to begin. It was not the real me who caused these horrible, tragic, and harmful events. It was the big bad wolf!

I must look deep into the eyes of the wolf through that mirror, and I must look long and hard and be brutally honest if I want to see it. It is there, and it is hiding, getting bigger, faster, and smarter. The wolf is waiting for me to take my eyes off it so that it may once again come and prey on the weak, the sick, and the weary.

I, as the sheep, must get past the past.

Insanity is doing the same thing and expecting different results.

It is time to step up as a lion. I must be honest, proud, courageous, and bold!

It is time to hunt the big bad wolf! The hunt will be long, violent, and bloody, and it will encompass feelings and emotions—depression, anxiety, and anger—that will try to stop me, confuse me, and derail me. They will all work in tandem to get my eyes off the big bad wolf to lose focus.

I must arm myself from myself.

I need a total surrender from this disease and any notions that it will prevail. This time, it needs to know it will die!

In my quiver, there are arrows of brutal honesty, fresh knowledge, support, and spiritual self-forgiveness.

Brutal honesty. True, gut-wrenching honesty hurts, but once it appears to me as my weapon and not my enemy, none are mightier.

Fresh knowledge. Knowledge is power. Self-affirmations and lessons, such as the cognitive behavior theory, help me map out the territory. They help me know where I am, know what I am going after, know what weapons I have to attack it with, and know that I am on track, constantly working out emotionally and mentally to prepare for the challenge ahead.

Support. Never go hunting alone. My wife flew in today to be at my side. She is the enemy of my disease. She has been the target for so many years of my anger. She is my lover, my hope, and my angel. As soon as I surrendered to my disease, it was as soon as she arrived. There she is, at my side, shoulder to shoulder, dropping her life and coming to my rescue to lead the support system that I must build. All sturdy, solid, and stable buildings are built with a strong cornerstone. She is my cornerstone, and I am proud to have her leading the team!

I thank you for your years of forgiveness and resilience. Help guide me through this tunnel toward the light, the light of hope, and toward renewed relationships. Help me track this creature in the dark, still, and creepy forest to hunt it down and kill it.

The kids, another integral part of my support system, also called me to check in today. They called me to say good night. Their words felt like a glass of warm, smooth, and rich hot chocolate on a cold winter night, cutting directly through the chill of my situation and warming my heart. Thank you, son. Thank you, daughter. I can't wait to meet you again for the first time—for the first time that I am the real me, not that monster you both have come to know, to fear, and to pray to do us more harm. We will hunt together in a pack and do unto it what it wishes to do to me.

Spiritual self-forgiveness. Forgiveness is essential—not from others, that is comforting, but from myself. I should stop beating myself up till I am just short of death. I should just stop and forgive but never forget. Use the past and those events that I can't control as tools of recovery. I need to stop using them as weapons of mass destruction against myself. I must sharpen this tool and aim it directly toward the throat of the disease and not be afraid to use it.

"The weak can never forgive. Forgiveness is the attribute of the strong" (Mahatma Gandhi).

I am afraid to look at the mirror. Will I be a sheep, or will I be a lion?

I am a lion. Hear me roar!

So off to this hunt and challenge I go, trying to avoid all the same pitfalls and traps.

There are so many more dangers that exist. What other big bad creatures live in the woods? Will I simply just fall prey to another, or will I be strong enough to have enough ammunition and to put myself into a secure-enough place so I will be safe from the creatures that prey on the sick?

I am anxious and excited; my heart is racing as if it is a car at the starting line of a race. My engine is revving, my brakes are ready to be released, and my entire car is shaking with anticipation. This race will be challenging. This race will be rewarding. This race just might save my life!

Godspeed!

I prepare to go to work on myself.

Am I prepared?

I open my tool chest, and I see that I only have two tools to work with for this job: my prayers and my rosary. These are two very powerful tools, but without other more dynamic tools, I will certainly fail. My faith is not concrete. I must abdicate my arrogance and my ego. I must reach out for help, pull over, and ask for directions. I must step into the uncharted waters of vulnerability and humility and try to find those individuals that may have the tools I need to succeed.

My entire life has been built around the notion of "plan the work, then work the plan!" This job will be no different, but this job is not the same, for I am not working for a paycheck. I am working for my life!

I want and need to get my life back. It is so much more valuable than what I have today—so, so, so much more valuable and priceless.

I miss myself. Hang in there. I know I am out there, and I am coming to get me!

The time has come to tear down the statue, smash the masks, get past my disease, and look in that mirror with brutal honesty. I must go find me. I must not look back, but I also must remember to never take my eyes off the big bad wolf.

I need to focus and be relentless on my journey. I must not forget about what this creature has done to me and, more importantly, to those around me. My disease will beg me to stop and to try to make

30   KEVIN KAMINSKI

me think that it was not that bad. My disease will lie. It will cheat. It will steal to get me back. So I must be bold and swift and keep being brutally honest. I must avoid the snags, the hazards, and the lies and to keep hunting until this coldhearted creature is no longer breathing.

There I am. I knew that I was there.

I am hungry, angry, lonely, and tired. I come out of the shadows and darkness of shame and guilt. Now I can be with those who truly want to help me, not those who want to just keep using me. I can allow them to feed me, calm me, hold me, and give me rest. I am out of the darkness and into the light. I can once again see the gift of life. I shall cherish it, embrace it, and never again take advantage of it.

I am still sick, but I am finally away from being alone with the creatures, and I can truly focus on the healing.

Welcome back me. I missed me!

I sincerely thank me for knowing when to *hunt or be hunted!*

Batten Down the Hatches

There is a storm coming upon this weathered, tested, and reliable ship. However, this time, unlike the others, I see the storm coming, and I have had the time to batten down the hatches.

I am taking the steps to prepare for the worst but to hope for the better. With preparation, there will be confidence; with confidence, there will be success!

Preparation is success!

Out with the old and in with the new.

Here is a quick summary of where I am at: It starts with recognition. I have come face-to-face with my disease, and it knows I see it and that I am coming after it. I have decided to be open and to finally take off the masks and get rid of my deceptive behaviors. I have questioned my motives, my true desires, and my inner being of brutal honesty. I am finally starting to hear, not just going through the exercise of listening. I am present, and I am enthusiastic, anxious, and scared. Emotions are being discovered—emotions and all the feelings that come along with them. My brain is clear and focused, like a sponge soaking up any and all knowledge thrown my way.

Knowledge and preparation are power!

I need more. I want more—more tools, more help, and more support— so that I may build shelter, find hope, and gain strength for the storm that is fast approaching.

I can't prepare the ship for this storm if I don't understand how this ship operates. If I am not prepared and fully aware of who, what, why, and where I am, then I don't know how to operate myself. And I will surely be a victim to another merciless storm. So I gain clarity and I gain confidence and I open up a manual that has never been opened before.

What do I do when my engine light comes on in my car?

What do I do when my ship acts up?

I open up the operating manual, and I learn about the problem at hand. Of course, it won't be that simple because my manual is like no other manual. It is my own personal manual. I am me, and I am an original, yes, one of a kind. So it is difficult to find the problems, the emotions, and the feelings that I have and need to discover. The learning is a step. It will open my eyes that have been closed, it will alert my ears that haven't been listening, and it will feed my mind that has been numb. I will unearth emotions and problems that I could never have imagined were real.

It's time to get my hands dirty, so I start dusting off my unused old owner's manual. I am going to open it up to page 1 and begin to attempt to discover what might be wrong and how to possibly fix it.

Boy, I am a complicated yet beautiful human being! This is well beyond my pay grade and skill level, so I will certainly need to get some assistance in trying to put this all together. If I take this apart, there is absolutely no humanly way possible that I could ever get it back together. I need someone that has seen this before, someone who has expertise in this arena. I don't need to nor do I have the time to reinvent the wheel. I need an experienced professional in this area to examine me and take a good look at what might be out of alignment.

This view of me will be of that from thirty thousand feet, like when I am skydiving. At the beginning of a jump, I need courage, strength, and boldness to jump out of the plane. (Some would say there is a fine line between bravery and stupidity.)

I need to take the first step. People always ask, "Why are you jumping out of a perfectly good airplane?" The answer is simple: I am not jumping for pleasure; I am jumping out of a plane that is going to crash.

I am jumping to save my life!

Against my human nature, I leap out of the plane. My body is in shock, and I can barely see and make out the landscape. The view is amazing, exhilarating, and jaw-dropping. I can see, but I can't make out the definition of where I am going to land. As my free fall progresses, my learning continues. I start to gain more clarity, and I can finally make out some of the good, the bad, and the ugly of the landing areas. All this sensory information is rushing by me as I fall, too fast to comprehend. It is all overwhelming. My heart is pounding, my blood is rushing through my veins, and all of me is present and buzzing with adrenaline, exactly like where I am at today—excited, anxious, and energized. I, too, am going too fast. I need to pull the rip cord for the parachute or else I will just continue this perilous fall to imminent death.

I pull the cord, and the parachute opens!

For a while now, I know that I am safe and I am not going to burn into the ground at terminal velocity. More amazingly, the parachute has slowed me down, and now all my senses can catch up to my surroundings and I can truly enjoy the marvel of what I am seeing, hearing, feeling, and learning. I am now much closer to the ground, and I have gained even more clarity. I can see the dangers, and more importantly, I can see the safe places to land. Now that I have slowed myself down, I can truly take the time to learn and to gain all the important knowledge to get me to where I want to go safely.

So here I am on this new path of recovery and discovery. I just jumped out of the plane. I am seeing myself from that thirty-thousand-foot view, and during this free fall, I will be learning and gaining self-confidence, self-awareness, and self-esteem. I sure do hope I have the will and intelligence to pull the rip cord when that time comes!

I am in a safe place—a place that understands that I am sick and that I have asked for help. I have reached out to grasp a safety rope. I have stopped to ask for directions. Although where I am at can't fix me, I am the only person, along with support, that has the ability and the will to accomplish that. This place, however, has an arsenal of weaponry, tools, and firepower to use and to discover to help me prepare for this challenge.

Preparation is knowledge. Knowledge is power.

Preparation is power!

These tools—these awesome, powerful, and thought-provoking tools—will allow me to open my mind and learn about myself. Like Charlton Heston's gun collection, it is an overwhelming display of firepower—firepower that ranges from small to big, old to new, and slow to fast. This place I am at has the same overwhelming collection of firepower, but these are not guns. They are the very tools that I will be able to use to prepare myself to be safe from the storm.

These are tools, such as the cognitive behavior theory, to imagine that I have thoughts that invoke feelings, which cause actions and lead to events—events that in my past cycle of addictive thinking would cause harm, pain, and destruction. This is a cycle that, if not broken, will surely end in eventual disaster and most likely death. Imagine being armed with the knowledge to be able to stop, think about the pattern, observe the possibilities, and then proceed to a safer, healthier action that just may end in a positive event (S-T-O-P). This is a cycle change that just might save my life!

Positive momentum, personal boundaries, recovery networks, building self-esteem and self-confidence, and my own creativity put a twist on some of these tools to help my mind figure it out and better comprehend.

Affirmations are both positive and negative. I should recognize the negative but reaffirm the positive with myself and, more powerfully, with others. Judgment, two days ago, was a piercing, evil, and wicked action. Yet today I am positively reinforcing judgment from these wonderful, trusted, and healing individuals who have been the very first to see me without my mask.

I have finally been able to take off my masks!

I am now vulnerable, afraid, and brutally honest. This is my worst nightmare realized, and yet what an amazingly powerful dream and fantasy come true.

I am still sick, but now I know it, and I can finally look into the mirror and see me. I can see that I am everything my disease has hidden from me. I can now begin to heal. All these are wonderful tools and guides to healthy life management.

It makes me wonder, Why do we have to wait till the storm is upon us and our ship has crashed upon the jagged reef's edge in order for us to obtain these tools? Why wasn't I armed with such powerful information as a young adult? Was it that I was invincible, on the rise, and successful so these ideals didn't relate to me? When I was healthy, I didn't have the desire or the need to reach out for any ropes or help. I didn't need help; I stood alone!

Like faith, it is so difficult to reach the healthy and the happy, but it is very easy to attract the sick and the sad. Desperation brings the need for help, and needing help brings the human ability to reach out and find it.

I must now be a beacon of light—the weathered old lighthouse that sits on the reef's edge to protect the tired, weary, and unaware travelers. I am a bright, shiny light!

Some days, I am visible for miles because those days, the weather is good, the ocean is calm, and no real danger exists. It is not these days that I must shine my brightest. It is when the howling winds, the driving rains, the dense fog, and the angry seas all join together as a symphony of destruction that I must shine my brightest. It is then that I must remember that even though I can barely be seen through the rage of the moment, I must remember I am still a bright, shiny light!

Remember that this storm will pass, this disease will be defeated, and once again, I will return to a serene environment. I must remember to always be preparing and to always be looking out for the next storm that will eventually come my way. I will succeed because I can now see the storm coming. I have my eyes firmly set upon it. I am also beginning to learn and understand this ship, and I have been preparing. I have taken this valuable time to *batten down the hatches!*

Metamorphosis and Rebirth

I feel like a butterfly, a large majestic monarch, that has been enclosed and captured in a dark, lonely cocoon. I am starting to break out of that cocoon and beginning to fly.

I do have some concerns and anxieties with the common notion of that which goes up must eventually come down. But the more and more I learn and reflect, I am truly starting to believe that I have lived my life so down emotionally that I am just finally starting to fly upward from the bottom and upward toward health, happiness, and awareness.

My life has also mirrored the life of the mighty phoenix. The phoenix begins its life at the bottom. It grows and matures over time. It then becomes a mighty, powerful creature that is on fire. Unfortunately, it burns out of control, and the fire overtakes the mighty creature. These unforgiving flames consume this once-proud, successful creature. Now the once-mighty phoenix is just a pile of ashes—a pile of lifeless, emotionless, and lost ashes. Then the miracle happens. The phoenix rises from the ashes of its past. It begins the cycle of learning and regrowing, and soon, it will soar again.

I am the mighty phoenix. I am climbing out of the ashes of disease and confusion. I am learning, I am growing, and soon, I will soar again!

But I am fully aware and I am ensuring that this time, I will not make the same mistakes and not follow the repetitive life of the phoenix. I will make the changes I have learned and have the courage to change them to protect myself from burning out of control.

> God, grant me the serenity to accept the things I
> cannot change,

The courage to change the things I can,
And wisdom to know the difference. (Serenity Prayer)

Yesterday, my goal was to forgive myself.

I did!

I was able to look into the mirror today without the heavy burden of the past staring back at me. I got to see me, and I actually smiled at myself. Of course, I immediately broke out in tears.

I can cry!

It seems that the tears of yesterday, those created by completely uncontrollable sobbing, released some of the toxins full of pain, anguish, sorrow, and regret. Those tears are now mere dried-up splotches on the tissues on my floor. These new tears are tears of joy, of hope, and of relief that a new day has dawned. The phoenix has risen. I have given myself an opportunity to heal, an opportunity to open up my wings and fly again.

Flying is so liberating. Flying is so mysterious. I am also very aware that flying is also very dangerous. Its danger increases if you don't pay attention to the alarms and the environment around you.

Danger is ever present but not always visible.

Boarding flight number "me," fasten your seat belts, please turn off all cell phones and outside distractions, and relax and enjoy the flight. I will get me safely to my final destination.

I had a clinical assessment today. I sat and tried to listen. I tried to keep my eyes open, my mouth quiet, my ears listening, and my body still. I could do none of the above. I was like a bad child interrupting and fidgeting throughout the visit. I listened to the outside world's snapshot of who I am. The assessment was full of judgment and incorrect assumptions. Roughly 70 percent of the story is what they have captured; the other 30 percent has been left to these misguided and judging minds to fill in for themselves. I must remember that they are here to help, they mean well, and they—like no other—have gotten to see the shaking, completely isolated, lonely, and vulnerable cocoon that I was when I arrived. They have given me an educated diagnosis—manic with bipolar tendencies is the conclusion, and to help treat this, they have suggested a medication.

I am nervous and scared!

I have finally discovered emotions and feelings—both of which I have spent years self-medicating with my addiction so I can mask them, hide them, and be ashamed of them and so I can ensure that they are never felt or dealt with. So why would I want to replace my addiction with medication to once again cover up and go numb to what I just discovered?

I am confused, and I am frightened.

I am being asked to replace one creature with another. I have seen this, I have heard of this, and I don't want this. They have ensured me that they just need to bring me out of the clouds and get me to a safer place—a slower and steadier mental place. They simply want to help me pull the rip cord on my parachute and slow myself down. I went ahead and followed their suggestions. It took great strength and faith, but I am now safely floating down, still in the sky but now able to navigate the landscape and enjoy the ride.

It is equally as joyful and rewarding to see those around me on their flights of health and freedom from their diseases. Smiles, laughter, joy, and hope are all present in these rooms today. These are all the emotions and actions that when I came in here I wasn't sure I would ever see again.

Yesterday, a little boy was visiting his healing grandfather to see his grandfather beaming and being present and shining so brightly. To see his grandson rolling around on the floor and giggling—how therapeutic this was.

When did we lose the ability to giggle?

What a powerfully healing sound! The simple sound of an innocence child's giggle.

My goal today is to try to giggle!

Today is also a changeover day. It is a very uncomfortable day. More and more cocoons arrive, all in the same dark, lonely, and desperate stage of their lives. The world is cruel, and the number of demons is great. The demons are preying and feasting on the weak and the weary every day. The world provides a plentiful, revolving, and abundant source of cocoons.

All are sick, but some are sicker than others.

Intertwined with these fresh cocoons are those that have been here and have begun to break out of their cocoons and are enjoying the feel of their unfamiliar wings and flying around joyfully. It is a very confusing arena.

The cocoons that have freshly arrived are so broken, hurting, and full of self-doubt and disease. They feel hopeless and lost. I want to jump up and run to their rescue. I want to be their rock and give them something solid to hold onto.

It is during this time that I experience yet another miracle! I am flying around as a butterfly, and I run into an ominous cocoon. It tells me its story. It is as if I am having yet another out-of-body experience. As I listen, it is as if I am in a movie and I have traveled back in time to exactly five days ago—to the day I arrived. Listening to its story, I sit bewildered, shocked, and grounded by the fact that it is *me*. I am getting an opportunity to see myself and what I was feeling five days ago—not on an audio tape or even a video tape but live, speaking with raw emotions and brutal honesty and physically scared, defenseless, and hopeless. I take a second to analyze its story and its snapshot of where it is at, and I am floored by what I discover. I would be willing to bet that 90 percent of this cocoon's story matches mine. It is shocking. It takes my breath away. This isn't just a cocoon. It is truly *me* in the past! Thank you, God, for this miracle. I have now seen my growth, and I have gained important positive momentum.

This cocoon, like myself at the time, is very sick. I want to jump into the turbulent seas, grab the cocoon, and swim it to safety. However, I must stop myself and remember that I am still sick. I am far from healed, and I need to continue to focus on myself. It pains me to not immediately jump in, but I know that I would only drown along with it. My mental and physical position is still too fragile, and it would be extremely dangerous for me to go back into the sea. I need to stay on solid ground. However, I feel stable enough to throw out a life raft. This life raft is in the form of hope and promise.

I return the favor and give the cocoon my story, my current journey, and the growth that I have experienced in such a short time. Then it happens, amazingly, right in front of my eyes. I see a crack, a definitive slice in its cocoon. Now I can see that my hope has given me the ability to see the beautiful butterfly that is tucked inside, still hurting and full of doubt. But what is more rewarding is that it can now see me! It is no longer in the dark, lonely cocoon. It can see the light! Remember that this isn't the light of an oncoming train but the light of the lighthouse, the light of hope and promise.

I am a bright, shiny light!

That is all I can do for these cocoons. I must be steadfast and focused, and I must continue steadily toward my goal. I am confident that just being a butterfly and flying around them will bring them hope, light, and faith, and they can begin to heal. Lead by example, but be aware of the boundaries.

Goodbye, darkness of the cocoon. This butterfly has morphed and is beginning to fly. This phoenix has been reborn! I have experienced *metamorphosis and rebirth!*

See You Again Someday

It is very interesting that during this entire journey so far, I have not once mentioned the outside world—my life, my family, my work, current events, weather, sports, emails, cell phones, friends, Facebook, and on and on and on. My life on the outside deals with each and every one of these plus a list ad infinitum.

The outside world—is it cloudy? Is it sunny? Is it hot or cold? Is it in chaos or at peace? Who is winning the game? Has everyone acquired "it"? Most of all, if I am in here, then who is in charge out there? For truly, without me in the world, there must certainly be riots, mayhem, and possibly, global shutdown. Just this morning, one of the new cocoons cracked, and some light shed in on this beautiful young butterfly. Shaking, scared, and vulnerable, it innocently asked, "How is the world going to be all right if I am in here and not out there taking care of it?" This was one of the exact same thoughts that I had, poisoning my mind when I first looked through the crack in my cocoon. Now a little wiser, a little stronger, and out of our cocoons, all the butterflies in the room—with our brand-new wings aimlessly flying around—responded to the new cocoon with "The last time we looked, the world is still here. Your name hasn't even been mentioned on the local news channel." So funny, so common, and so sad that I also find myself believing that the world revolves around me.

Remember, this is all because of that overinflated and out-of-control ego—the ego that continues to be a creature that lives in the woods and has joined up with my disease. My ego continues to be extremely dangerous. When I came in here, I was an arrogant, selfish, and self-centered SOB. Now that I have been in here a few days, I am still an arrogant, selfish, and self-centered SOB, but now, I know I am and I can begin to change that.

Why can't I stop my ego from writing checks that my ass can't cash?

Can I please check my ego in at the door?

If it has to come with me, I will be a ship that leaves port but forgets to lift its anchor, moving forward but moving very slowly and often getting stuck emotionally and physically, not to mention damaging and destroying the enchanting ocean floor. Some of these damages will be unfixable, leaving ugly and lasting scars that will always be there so that the damages will never be forgotten.

We all have an ego. The goal is to keep it in check and to attempt to not let it rule our world. I love the acronym EDGING GOD OUT. That puts my ego in its place and lets me know exactly how and whom I need to defend against it. I must use God, my higher power, to assist me in shrinking my ego each and every day. I must break up the alliance that it and the addiction have formed.

But nonetheless, I am out of the hustle and bustle of the world. It was a life-changing and lifesaving event five days ago when I made the decision to pause my world and finally take a break—a time-out to take care of me, myself, and I, a complete and total immersion into my health and recovery, taking away all extractions, turning down the volume, and getting away from the noise so that I could focus on gathering information and knowledge about what I am going through.

Knowledge is power!

I am the phoenix rising up from the ashes, but my life path was a little different. I was certainly caught up in the flames and was on my way to being consumed by them. I was able to extinguish the flames before I burned my life into total ashes. Plenty of my life was burned up, and it lay in ashes, but some of my life survived the fire. I was able to get off the elevator before it went all the way to the basement.

Remember, on August 22, 2013, I was given a gift—a very special gift that reminds me of when I was a young child on Christmas morning, eager and excited about what Santa Claus just might have left under the tree for me. I would sneak downstairs and search under the Christmas tree for that gift, that special gift.

My special gift!

I would finally find it, and I would do the crazy, silent, happy dance that I did when I was a kid. Then I would have to wait and wait and wait for what would seem like a lifetime for my parents to wake up so that we could open our presents.

Just like that Christmas gift I was given, I had to wait almost three decades to receive this gift. But when it came, it hit me like a bolt of lightning—a bolt of lightning that took me to my knees and completely knocked the breath out of me. This bolt of lightning jolted my mind, my body, and my soul.

It was a gift that may just save my life!

The gift was one of complete mental clarity. When it hit me, my mind went through a flashback—a horrible, selfish, and dishonest flashback of all the events that my disease hid from me. I was able to see the path of destruction that my disease was laying down. It was amazing, it was horrifying, and it was incredibly enlightening. This gift was a miracle. It was all my fears realized—actual fears, not the ones my mind conjured up. This was more than any healthy mind could conjure up. This was more than any healthy mind could handle, so imagine what it did to my sick, troubled mind. The miracle of clarity.

I ask myself, "Why did I have to get hit with such a tremendous bolt of lightning and get caught in the perfect storm in order to recognize my problems?" Was it because I didn't feel the little lightning strikes that have been hitting me over the years? I was so sick and so self-absorbed that it took this type of storm to blow me off course and take notice. I believe that for years, God, my higher power, was trying to get my attention by hitting me with a ball-peen hammer, but my ego and self-centered lifestyle absorbed these taps and plowed on. It took a smack from a sledgehammer directly to my skull in order to get my attention. And boy did it!

Do you believe in miracles?

Well, I do. I was just given one. Now it is up to me to use it for the good and to take the experience, strength, and hope to get me over the next hurdles in life and to get my train back on the track of life.

I have grown a lot in this place, and I am ready to take off from this safe haven and to plug back into the matrix, back into the "real world," out of the confines of this safe, serene, and protected place—a place where the only thing I had was me to focus and work on, an excellent place to help begin the process of healing.

I believe anybody who has the courage and the time, no matter what their situation in life is, would benefit from stopping and taking a time out to help let their mind, body, and soul take a break. It is very relieving and revealing.

I get closer to the time that I will be leaving—leaving those individuals who, just a few short days ago, were complete strangers and a mystery to me. Today they are close acquaintances and people whom I feel I have known for a lifetime because they can relate to me and my disease. They, too, are sick. These are the individuals who were the first to see me without my mask, and I was able to see them without theirs. We were all able to let down our guards and just be our sick, vulnerable, and confused selves. It has been like watching a newborn baby colt trying to get up and walk for the first time. It starts confused and a little scared. It is extremely awkward yet excited. At first, it stumbles, but then it gains a few steps of momentum, and it endures the trials and tribulations of this new life event until it is successful. I, too, will be successful. I just have to remember to keep my eye on the woods, keep enduring, and never give up.

These connections that have been formed have such depth and closeness due to the relationships being formed under such intense pressure, similar to coal turning into a diamond. We started out as lumps of coal, but with the pressure, we have turned out to be beautiful colorful diamonds. Sure we have our flaws, but the clarity of the stones makes up for them. I have touched these individuals and been a part of their journey, and more importantly, they have touched me not physically but deeply in the form of mental and emotional encouragement. I feel like I have gained new brothers, sisters, aunts, and uncles.

They are a real, engaged, and dynamic family of priceless diamonds.

Take my hand, and I will take yours. Remember, we go nowhere unless we take the first step!

So off I must race into the rush-hour traffic and plug back into life and the fast and the furious and unforgiving pace of the outside world. I will be like a dog on the highway—heart racing, head spinning, and nerves on edge. Which way do I go? Where do I turn? What next? I have an overload of senses—a complete and total overload of a once-calm nervous system. There are cell phones, texts coming and going, clocks, traffic, meetings to organize and run, family issues, kids stuff, relationships to handle and heal, friends calling to get the 411, people judging, and people calling to be nice (but really only judging and prying). On top of all this madness and insanity, I am still sick. I am far from healed. I am only at the very beginning of this journey. I have been able to admit that my life is unmanageable and that I am powerless. I have surrendered to my illness and reached out for help. I have a very long and difficult challenge ahead. I am not only a dog. I am an injured dog on the highway of life.

But I am one of the lucky dogs in this transition period, for I have chosen to continue my path of recovery. I only have to endure all this madness and reality for just one night. I get to continue to work on myself and grow stronger and smarter so that I can defeat this disease. I will seamlessly be going to another intense and focused institution to continue to gain the weapons and strength that I will need to defeat this illness and regain my life.

It is sad to listen to the others struggling to know what will be next in their lives, considering so many complications and restraints. Jobs, families, and friends are all roadblocks to recovery. There are unknown paths and dangers around every corner and pitfalls to be navigated—all while disease lurks and grows in the dark forest.

Who's afraid of the big bad wolf, the big bad wolf, the big bad wolf?

Now imagine a dozen scared, startled, and injured dogs on that busy highway—a complete set up for a tragic and bone-shattering accident. It pains me to know that not all these dogs will make it to their final destinations. Accidents will happen, dogs will get lost, and worst of all, some dogs may die.

Am I the dog that gets hit in the traffic?

Self-doubt creeps in. The disease is again reaching out with its claws trying to pull me back into its darkness and control.

No, I am not the dog that will get hit! For once again, I don't have to cross the road yet. I only have to change kennels. I will be exposed to very little danger, risk, and reality. That doesn't mean that they don't exist and aren't out there waiting for me, hiding around the corners and lurking in the woods. But remember, I see it, and I have the focus today to be intelligent enough, calm enough, and sturdy enough to keep my eyes on it so that it can't cause a surprise attack.

It truly has been amazing to me—the amount of growth that I have felt in my early stages of recovery. It is amazing to be able to recognize the problems, the emotions, and the feelings and to learn how to react to them and more importantly, how they interact with me. So far, I have been hunting with a trusty old shotgun. With a shotgun, it is easy to hunt small game, birds, and inanimate objects such as clay. This institution has aided me in steadying my hands, focusing my sight, and hitting the targets. So watch out, disease, because you are the target, and I am going to hit you dead center. I have my eyes and my sights set square on you. But I am smart enough to know if I go hunting a wolf with a shotgun that will not work, and eventually, the wolf will defeat me. It knows that, and more importantly, I know that, so my illness is beginning to get nervous.

I know that all I have is a shotgun in my arsenal, and I will not go out to hunt with that alone. I need a bigger gun with a considerably increased amount of power, skull-rattling ammunition, and a very dense and focused target zone. I need a powerful rifle!

Where I am heading, there is an arsenal—an arsenal that is full of weapons that are exactly what I am looking for. They will be able to provide me with this type of weapon and its owner's manual. I know the target, so now I can take the time to focus on it. I am going to stop the process of ready, fire, aim. I am going to slow down, observe, and take it all in—the wind, the obstacles, and the distance. I will practice with this gun, sight it in, go to the range, and make sure I am getting a consistent grouping of shots.

I will spend the appropriate amount of time to take good care of this gun. I will clean it regularly, mentally, and physically. I want to ensure that nothing, and I mean nothing, shall lower my chances of success.

Ready, aim, breathe, shoot!

I am going to make sure that if I get a shot at it someday, it will be a lethal-kill shot.

I like guns. I love their power, but I must respect them and make sure that I do what is necessary so that they won't harm me. I am nervous and eager to get this gun, learn all about it, and most of all, get the chance to begin to fire it.

I have been extremely focused and been working incredibly hard to keep advancing my knowledge and skills to be learning more and more every day about what it will take to win this challenge. It is as if my mind is a combustible engine. Gas, spark, fire, explosion, piston up . . . gas, spark, fire, explosion, piston down . . . gas, spark, fire, explosion, piston up . . . gas, spark, fire, explosion, piston down. I feed the engine and its moving parts with inertia and move it forward, first very slowly but rapidly gaining pace. Each explosion is a thought, a memory, a moment in time going off in my mind and filling the empty pages. I am alive and clear minded, but I must remember to keep my eyes on the road. If I go too fast, I will increase my chance of running into trouble and getting into a wreck. I must use my brakes, keep it in low gear at first, and rev up the engine so that it doesn't stall out. I must be very careful not to run it at six thousand revolutions per minute for too long. If I do, there is an increased chance that it might blow up. The proper medication, the new knowledge, and the focus all act as the braking system for my engine. I have now left the starting line. The green flag is waving, and the race is on. This race will not be a drag race. It will be a long-distance endure—a grueling, lengthy, and very dangerous enduro.

Five days ago, I checked myself in to begin this journey away from the outside world. It has been five days since—fresh air, sunshine, rain, stars and clouds, aimless and refreshing walks, music, family and friends, pets, fluffy pillows, and exercise. However, I feel healthier and stronger and more alive than I have ever felt in my entire life.

"Float like a butterfly, sting like a bee" (Muhammad Ali).

I am baffled and amazed but still fearful of the rosy glasses and the pink cloud. Both are negative thoughts that my disease continues to try to shove down my throat to choke me up. But I am strong! I am healthy! I am alive!

I am now a participant in yet another absolutely beautiful phenomenon! As I prepare myself to leave this place, mystery and wonder are racing through my mind—good anxiety, exciting anxiety. Yet there is also sadness, a deep feeling and aching sadness that I will be leaving the butterflies that I have morphed with. I will be leaving the garden of healing and flying away. These are not goodbyes but see-you-laters, always leaving hope and the possibility that our paths may cross again in life but without expectations so that we don't cause any unexpected resentments. Then there are tears, not tears of sorrow and remorse, but good tears, the emotional big wet tears that help flush away the toxins. The wave of emotions crash into me, sending shivers down my spine. It feels like a bomb of a wave at the Banzai Pipeline crashing down on the steady, alert, and engaged surfer. I know it is coming, just as the surfer does, so all I can do is hold on and brace myself for the overwhelming slam of the wave of emotion.

I can cry, and I do!

It is hard, very hard. It is much more difficult than I would have ever expected five short days ago. Once again, I reflect on how tight the bonds that were formed here were. Diamonds, precious and rare diamonds.

But I am suddenly startled and in a panic. I have given my last messages of hope to all the butterflies and cocoons, all the diamonds, except one, a very, very special diamond to me, for it is me in the future. Another time-travel miracle, I have been given the foresight and ability to shake my own hand in the future. I am shaking with fear and excitement. I finally find this special diamond—the one that represents a future me.

See you later, me. Thanks for reaching for the rope and for stopping to ask for directions and for taking off your mask. We are going to be all right. We are going to heal, and I am so proud of us because we took the first step.

Together, never alone!

Now I can be certain and I can guarantee that I will see this diamond in the future, for it is me!

As I reflect back on this scene, I can't help to see some confusion from the readers as to why I would be so happy to see myself in the same broken state after so many years. That, to me, is the point that is the strongest because I have been given the miracle to see what I could have been if I didn't make the change! I will be playing and doing the same old song and dance, driving into the tunnel, and waiting to crash into the train. How beautiful to know today that I have made a life-changing decision. The diamond I have met is me as an object, a thought. But now I have interrupted the cycle of self-destruction, and I am no longer circling around the sink, heading directly down the drain. I have interrupted that cycle and not reversing its momentum but going in the same cycle, only this time going outward toward the open space, toward a future of hope and endless opportunities. The sky is the limit, and I am flying. After a meaningful embrace, a solid handshake, and then the moment of separation, remember, this is not goodbye, but rather, *see you again someday!*

Transition

It is now time to leave this place and step through the doors of reality in order to get to my next destination. It is time to transition between here and there, yet I am still not going toward my final destination in life.

My wife comes through the doors and picks me up. I am lighter. I bounce like Tigger, and I am like a small rambunctious, questioning child. I am almost too much for my wife who has been living in the chaos without a break.

Then there is a kiss—not the first kiss but a kiss that has been sealed behind the mask for so many painful years.

I can cry!

I am now at the front desk, preparing to exit. Here, they hand me back my belt. It is another powerful gesture to the open and absorbing mind. It is simply a dull, ordinary transaction to my closed and numb mind of days ago; however, today I see it as a symbol of my caretakers gifting me another tool, another idea to have my mind grab it with its ridiculous appetite and to consume it like a pig at its trough. The belt to me is a symbol of security. I have been safe and secure with them in this serene environment. Now I am going out of their care and protection. My belt will wrap around me. It will secure my shorts, and it will hold me together. More whimsical symbols are coming from an overly alert mind that is ready for more.

"Feed me," grunts the pig!

I walk out of this sanctuary. I get my label off. For the first time in a week, I am not a lab rat in an experimental lab. I am no longer being judged. I am once again a normal member of our society with no obvious differences or glaring abnormalities.

I am lifted and given positive affirmations to lead me off toward this challenge. I reenter the world, plug back into the matrix, and like that wave of emotion from earlier, the overwhelming and overpowering thought of being in the ocean—swimming away from the ship, swimming away from stability, serenity, comfort, and safety toward the unknown, the chaos, the stress, and the danger—comes. However, I must also remember toward a new life, buried treasures, and hope eternal.

The wave of emotions once again crashes violently into the sandy shore.

I can cry!

My rock, my angel, my wife reaches out with open, inviting arms, gives me a hug, calms my beating heart, and most importantly, takes my hand.

Take my hand, and I will take yours! Let us take these first steps together. I must remember that I am never alone!

One foot in front of the other, slowly, I must crawl before I can walk and walk before I can run. I don't charge out into the world like William Wallace in *Braveheart* into battle. I go out cautiously, like a buck walking into an open meadow. Aware, alert, and slow, I enter into life, always observing, scanning the horizon, and keeping my eyes—my no-longer-blind eyes—in the direction of the woods and directly into the dark, lifeless, doll eyes of the wolf!

I am a hunter, and I will succeed!

I notice everything, and I mean everything. My eyes are looking and actually seeing, my nose is smelling, my ears are listening and actually hearing, my mouth is tasting, and my body is feeling, such as the feeling of a caring, loving, and forgiving touch from my wife. My body at first flinches and is startled. I have not really been touched in almost a week. I have been in isolation from physical contact—again all a part of the time-out. Any physical contact could have possibly caused me to lose focus, to take my eye off the wolf. So when the touch comes, it comes expectantly unexpected. Hence, chills shoot straight down my spine and the hair on my arms and neck stand up straight like a battalion of soldiers standing at attention. It is electrifying, and it was undeniably missed. I ponder, When was the last time I truthfully felt?

Just a week ago, I could touch, but I was numb. Therefore, I could not really feel.

Then there is the fresh air, the smell of a garden, the sound of music, the heat of the sun. The sun is a bright, shiny light, then there is the fresh air, the smell of a garden, the sound of music, the heat of the sun. The sun is a bright, shiny light beaming its rays of nourishing vitamin D down into my body and soul.

I missed you, sun, I have been under the cover of clouds—black, stormy, and ominous clouds that came in with the storm that hit five days ago, the scariest storm I have ever had to sail through with striking lighting, driving rains, fifteen-foot waves, and hurricane-like winds. But there was a silver lining in those clouds. The storm blew me off course, and it interrupted my self-destructive cycle.

This storm just may have saved my life!

I am now sitting at the airport, sitting in the corner, once again watching and reading this story that is pouring out of my buzzing with movement. Hundreds of ideas and thoughts scatter about, and I am attempting to organize them and load them onto their correct flights so they will arrive at their final destinations.

The thoughts and words that are flowing out of my overactive mind are painting such a stunning portrait of this moment in time, a portrait of who I am.

Who am I?

I see my wife. She looks alarmed. What has happened? She is panicked, for she has been searching for me for over an hour. I have accidentally sat at the wrong gate! My poor angel, such a simple mistake on my part and I have made her panic. I could only imagine what was going through her racing mind, for it was not but just a short two hours ago she found me, I mean, found and saw me—not the me that has been sealed in that cocoon of disease, not the me that has been behind that mask of deception, but the me that can be loved, the me that won't start a fight over the smallest of things, the me that is vulnerable and fragile. The me that can cry.

I can cry!

So my poor wife searches and searches like a stray dog trying to find a loving, caring, and secure home and family. She sees my light, she runs over, and we embrace and feel each other's heartbeats both racing—hers because of panic and mine because of the anxiety of what lies around the corner of life. I am ready to board another flight, this time, a flight that I am not at the controls of, remembering yet again that I must let go of the wheel and trust that my captain will get me to my destination safely.

The flight attendants have gone through their preflight program, the engine is revving, the brakes are released, and we are speeding down the runway. Then there is that awkward and startling feeling of the wheels leaving the ground.

"Please remain seated with your seat belts fastened. There are some storms ahead, and the ride may get a little bumpy."

In my mind, I think, *Stormy and bumpy . . . I'm telling you they sure are coming. Yes, they are. If they only knew the size and strength of the storms that are coming my way.*

We reach the cruising altitude of thirty thousand feet, and the *bing* of the seat-belt signs rings out. I unbuckle my seat belt. I sure am glad they taught me how to do that for the one thousandth time in my life. Without that knowledge, I may have been stuck there forever. Still sarcastic, a hard pill to swallow, I get out of my seat. I am leaving security once again, taking a little more risk, inviting possible danger into my life. However, I do a quick risk-reward table, and I sense a relatively small chance for danger versus the fact that I need to go to the lavatory really bad. Nature calls, and I see nothing but reward in this scenario.

I walk cautiously up the aisle, shifting on my feet as the airplane jostles around because of some mild turbulence, and I safely reach the lavatory. I enter, I lock the door behind me, and the light flickers to life. I drop my drawers, very vulnerable and awkward in these not-so-spacious accommodations. I sit and *zap!* Something bites me right in the ass! With shock and awe, I am startled, my heart is pounding, and my blood is pumping. The toilet seat happens to be cracked, and the exposed jagged edge takes an unanticipated bite out of my buttocks!

Am I in immediate danger? No! But I am playfully reminded that surprises and the unknown are out there, everywhere. They are lurking around the corner, hiding in the dark, spooky, and dangerous forest, so I must always be aware and I must keep my guard up.

During this break, I get a second to sit and reflect—reflect on a bathroom similar to this one on the plane, the bathroom in the institution that I was just at for the last week. One would say that it was quite dull and lifeless—blank white walls and no hooks or hangers.

Many readers have got to be wondering, "Where is this going?"

Back in my bathroom, it had a shower, a toilet, and really not much more. It was boring and serene but very useful and effective. There was no outside static to distract the mind. It was very simple and quiet. Yet every time I would step into that space, it was as if my mind would launch into an orbit of ideas, like a rocket leaving the launch pad at NASA.

"Systems checked, all systems go, commencing countdown. T-minus ten, nine, eight, seven, six . . . main engines, ignite . . . five, four, three, two, one! Blast off!"

The rocket starts to shake and tremble and slowly at first moves upward, gaining more and more speed as it lifts off, leaving an unbelievable path of smoke behind it. It leaves the launchpad. The astronauts voice says, "Houston, we have lifted off."

But wait, no celebration at ground control. Those watching the controls are watching and aware of everything going on with the rocket. They know how it operates inside and out. On a sidenote, could you imagine the size and scope of that owner's manual? They are alert and aware and keeping their eyes on the rocket and watching for any alarms or warning signs—alarms such as bells, whistles, beeps, and buzzes. Ground control is highly aware that this rocket is not yet out of danger; in fact, it is like during the free fall. It is moving so fast that the danger is in fact at its highest point, so the focus must be at its peak.

I am focused!

As the rocket reaches its stride, it has gotten past the intense area of danger. We hear the voice of the astronauts. "Houston, we have a successful launch"

Celebration erupts! High fives, hugs, and rejoices flow out of the ground control like lava out of an erupting volcano. Now moving on to the next stage of the mission. But wait, if you look more closely at the control room, you will notice that not all controllers are distracted and celebrating. There is always a number of controllers keeping an eye on the rocket, for it is never out of danger. I have my eyes on the danger as well. I am using this relentless practice of keeping myself aware and alert for my alarms. Nonetheless, like the rocket, after I have entered into my bathroom, my mind goes into orbit—open and flowing with ideas. All these ideas are made up of brutal honesty and raw emotions. They need to leave my mind, and they become these stories. They flow out of my mind like undammed tears flowing from my broken heart! These feelings and thoughts once again remind me that I am still alive, I am human, and I am beginning to heal. I have named my bathroom the think tank. It is where most of this journey has been incubated.

I finish my business and return to my seat. I am now back in my seat, buckled back into security, and I am once again cruising along at thirty thousand feet. I gaze out the window and try to make out the landscape below. I am way too far up to make it out. The good news is that I am not jumping out of this perfectly good airplane, nor am I landing near our current location. I don't have to worry about gaining any knowledge. I can relax and trust in the pilot's knowledge and skills. All I need to do is enjoy the flight.

A few hours later, we begin to make our descent, slowly and in control and making sure to keep our eyes on the horizon.

"We will be landing shortly. Please make sure your seats are in their upright position and all of your carry-ons have been stowed properly."

The ground then begins to approach. Where is the airport? Where is the safe landing area? Closer and closer to the ground—finally, the runway appears. There is some relief, but we are still moving at a very fast and dangerous speed. Closer and closer and then *bang*! It is a rough and violent landing. The passengers gasp, their hearts beat faster, and there is the sound of a child's giggle.

After this event, this unleashed mind's engine revs up again.

Isn't it amazing that one event, the rough landing in this case, could illicit two incredibly polar responses that result in two totally different feelings? The wiser older passengers feel fear then relief from the rough landing. The innocent young child feels excitement and joy. They giggle because that child's innocence doesn't realize that there is any danger whatsoever. This goes the same in life. The more we learn, the more knowledge we acquire. This can work for us and sometimes against us. Here is just one example of how knowledge can be negative and positive. It is negative because we know about the fear and the dangers of the situation. It is positive because since we know there are dangers, we can keep our eyes focused on them and be prepared for them. I don't care either way, but in this instance, it sure would be nice to be the child and to be able to giggle in the face of danger.

We have landed safely, and the trust that I have placed in the pilot has paid off. I look forward to deplaning and going to my next destination.

We are now off the plane, and we need to take a short train trip to the baggage claim. I grab on to the safety strap because I have the knowledge of how this train reacts. I am prepared for the storm. My wife grabs and hugs me. Like clockwork, the train lurches ahead, and my wife's embrace quickly tightens. This tight embrace brings on the intense feelings of love and security and togetherness.

This train trip will be short, but the journey that I have ahead will be very, very long. I am well on my way. I am in *transition*.

Made in the USA
Monee, IL
09 February 2020